HALLUCINATION

WILLIAM FULLER

HALLUCINATION

FLOOD EDITIONS

2011

Published by Flood Editions

www.floodeditions.com

ISBN 978-0-9819520-7-9

Design and composition by Quemadura

Printed on acid-free, recycled paper

in the United States of America

This book was made possible

in part through a grant from

the Illinois Arts Council

"The (Tendentious) Spirit" was adapted

from Robert Fludd's manuscript

The Philosophicall Key, as transcribed

by Allen G. Debus in *Robert Fludd and*

His Philosophicall Key (New York:

Science History Publications, 1979).

Some poems in this book have

previously appeared in *The Canary*,

Chicago Review, *Dear Navigator*,

Lifecoach, *The Nation*, and *Wig*.

Love, that is blood within the veins of time

FOR ELIZABETH

FOR THE VOID / 1

1

2

3

HALLUCINATION

FOR THE VOID

My eyes close: horse, dog, monkey gather together at wood's edge—to observe one another, make sounds, drink juice, pour down salt. The primitive nature of this scene evokes deep memories of crude states, before the imposition of trembling, paleness, and sobbing. As I will show

1

OK JAZZ FUNERAL SERVICES

I see you everywhere and I like you everywhere
and my location in any sentence
depends on the objects surrounding
you, and they're not you, and you're not them
and we, all of us, surround ourselves according
to the disappointments we distill
as we approach the end—
here's a set of principles shaped like a plane
flying low over the city
it looks like a clarinet—
give me my ticket and my
tangled red hair and my green
coat and my purple hand-knit scarf
and also my
glasses

scum on the cemetery pond, high barbed wire,
crenellations, Cornelia, Cordelia, Roscoe, Prospero
there's trash in the yard
parked over there
the banjo player and the banjo know it
autonomous relationships are included
twice
trailing off (we
possess the expression
whether pretending to grasp

details
think propose discuss decide abandon
not that they know
whose flesh it is—

I have no blood inside my brain tonight
I think there's a caterpillar who suggests
the first thought that comes to me
and stands firm through the chaos
as it enters the room—
I see a cost structure made of stale cornbread
minus two percent
I want the two percent living, sane, and saying something
richer, deeper
I sleep
in the clean white studio of the morning sun
with vast blue palaces of space
stuffed into my head
they float exceptionally well
offering no explanation except speech
itself a sphere, enclosing birds
who listen out of strangeness
then posthumously descend
great flocks of them
migrating nine miles
through a silvery drainpipe
to the demonstrated absence of a material fact—
hence these baskets

Simon Templao
untied the mooring line and drifted away
the dogs barked out a distant thumping
to the candles of guitars
reflected in his duck-shaped spoon
dimly through sand and deeply through streams
a robin
flung droplets
                    in arcs
winding through the porcelain eye
singly or antecedently
joined together by streaming threads
a golden few, now retired
their arms bent like backbones
their bamboo legs clattering
against a fragrant bowl
and plucked—

the foregoing is not possible
in the glaucous east bright alpha
indescribably substantiates
the work of hands
hammered into coins—
daylight
coordinates their circulation
among a privileged class of seekers
which grabs its feet and smacks its nose
renewing deep rifts and heavy deletions

for now he's arrived
and these
are his

I remember the day my transmission died
over there stood three red stools
people gathered on the roof to watch
sweeter as the years go by
in bursts of gray light
on the surface of the sun—
think of your policy man, think of his pitch,
think of what you suddenly notice
when you look downstairs,
downstairs
think of the concourse
the claves, the trombone, the bedsprings
of the chief musician
on Neginoth
think of the gusts of rain or the law of retaliation
when it's dark
and where isn't it
I wish someone would tell me

ON THE SUPERNATURAL

This is a sign formed of a tear attached to a pole representing an entire day. It has a separate existence like the eagle. Who would surrender a king because he dresses differently in front of a little mirror? The light in the window is far larger than the earth. Tucked away in expressive devices, stars flow into common fields along both axes, then weaken and long to return. I argue that work performs a supernatural act or is an elaborate brief for the next supernatural act: demonstrable, persuasible, opinionable, ostensibly believed. Time dries out the brain. While I am stuck in fire. And dominoes. The voice is sadder, more resigned; others are propping it up, or its empirical equivalent—whereas we have no sensation. Out of the center a gap is struck. The gap defines what cannot change, but hears deeply, correctly, and if it resembled trees or streets all corresponding signs would conform to them in the listener's mind. Drinking watery foam, touching limits of a formal and fantastic character, the soul arises unstrung to calculate the breadth of undivided space. One day the Lifeless, Mechanical, and Contrived will join opposites in unity. More marvelous. More beautiful. Leaping across aroused streams. Neither impossible nor incredible, you are a cold wind on a sunny day, somehow composed of things.

EASTERN SLOPE

pale plaintiff seeks snap to her
      gait
so she abandons me without
      no action
who'd pardon a true lover of the
      thieving art
owner of sod farms, tree farms,
      piping
the whole social order; it
      doesn't apply—
we are bumps on a wave
      viviparous
causing tears no graphic
      talent
can mask, in contempt
      of content
green skies approach, the price
      soars, so,
subject parcel strikes bird
      it makes no
sense, he simply went nuts
      as you see
the fund is closed but the beast
      still adores you

THE (TENDENTIOUS) SPIRIT

The (tendentious) spirit dispersed through the vaines, arteries and contemporary

mining

segment

doth provoke and stir up Status Real on every side & sustayneth the lumpe or mass of the body uprightly like a Winged Quadruped. Therefore wee see that ther is no element in the corporall and visible matter (or similar hypostatic continuum), but hath transacted in the same kind with a spirituall substance which doth regulate it, neyther is ther any subordinating assignment of materiall or formal Pyramis below the spheare of the sonne (to be redeemed at cubick par), but hath the selfe same image or forme above the sonne, ascertainable by reference to pre-empted volumes of space. The fatal difference being [that] the lower part of the world is materiall (the junco), whereas the upper part is spirituall (the nuthatch). Whereby it is evident that as the soule is the exponent of the spiritual Kinge so is the body the hurdle rate of the soule, being it is adapted to be the suitcase thereof, but her parts are more grosse and visible, for Hermes Trismegistus teacheth us that, that which is gross is as that which is subtill, and that which is subtill is as that which is gross. And these together equal No. Thus we have heaven uppon earth & earth upon heaven, thus we have againe heaven within earth & earth within heaven, & by consequence earth and heaven ar nothing else but one thinge which is water. Milky water, smooth and deep, coating every cell with standby assurances, a third of them in words.

JELLON GRAME

all split sky scrapes me
moiety
light grass and jersey frere
disentangle
street becomes becalmed
in a plume of clear plastic
omit yourself
and arise arise
tawny epithets
to brace these gates
full of great doors
leaking blood
at half-past seven
it was springtime
and the broadside
ate your meal
eastward circling
like the overhang of
so much gesture
based on receipts
rain-soaked feet
pour down—
why is it something
for him to look
epigrammatic
always at dawn

flakes pinpoint
the escutcheoned
shed

spaces for arches
                    disembark
trip trial pandemic
drill motile mass
split robot fiber
brine basal chord

feathers trembling in bare trees
and out-of-phase abundance
create neural events
inevitably broken amen

drunk with brightness
my senses are insane
parked on a slant
you are the most
peculiar
snow
I've ever dreamed
emong the wind-up
p-powder
conjure what's next
slight air and purging fire
bent unquenched
against the jerk the stroke

the pomegranate—
teacher   had you decided
to withdraw from
immediate impressions
squinting as you tucked away
the paper—how beautiful
to hear it recited—why do
the night-loving roof-clingers rage?
spend your money please
it is full of mixture

EATING GRASS

is that
what you wish
innumerable hands
working the sieve
though I might only talk
others rise up
to throw oranges
or cut skin
to designate
the willow and the crane
practically shouting
their entrances
each grows more specific
and would prescribe new governance
but time is short
to teach the mind
a canticle
electrified
of dead branches
hanging low
in the morning
they speak
but we're working
if the intimation is otherwise
check with reason
alone in the clouds
or sprawling in your hair

the planet moves
biologically compromised
by our original relation
to ourselves
can you recognize us
in the red liquor
what is it to be stuck
under sky
who is
set up from everlasting
on a crowded street
a man strapped to a wall
a wall supporting a chimney
a bridge over the rails
heads moving below
trumpets—
what exactly intersects
ungrateful apparition
who can wander without end
where hundreds blossom
circularly jointed for motion
revolving
to the incomprehensible simplicity
of early light
from which spring
S-shaped breezes
uncoiling
the sun
at length magnified
sumac glows

G ____ P ___ , KUNG FU

The regular daily charter tipped forward to get new orders from those buying feed to stuff through keyholes (he asked for 10% of it), which are just visible peeking through the flexible mountings horizontally transformed by stone, rocks, and pebbles (why didn't he follow up?). In this space a dilemma is presented by the temptation to play the instrument into an expectancy, or flash those charismatic warning lights drivers ignore, transfixed by the intermittent wipe function. And George was also there to gather plums. Where was his toothache, Kung Fu? Why are his hands bound with iron rings? At dockside, dog-faced dealers strive to accommodate unexpected demand (shown here in component form). But while our whole future quivers on a shell, the fallacies from which our opponents derive themselves will be revealed atop the holy hill, at three o'clock, next Thursday, and continuing on through all the countless Thursdays until, lifted up on soft breezes, the trance-subject barks at acorns as they smack off the roof. See the birds of the air, how they overflow. George leans back at exactly the wrong time and enfeoffs his esophagus. His porcelain soul, subject to annihilation, adheres to uneven surfaces as a faint residual pulse beats out similes and parables. So much mental strain cannot help but manifest itself. We write a tortured letter. We quote a wounded argument. By default we gain possession of the field. Note the kind of eye given to this sight. We fold our hearts through a pinhole, Kung Fu. Do not increase or decrease these medicines I am recommending.

EARTHLY EVENTS

windy streets received
by the eyes
and a third face
crowded with faces
of whatever species
to which
the windy *gaudium* returns
topped with hair
what light
above below
nether sky
or twin skies
whitewashed hills
a sympathetic combination
of bare trees and stiff grass
the atmosphere
dense from the ambiguity of
words used to name it
now a curtain of cloud lifts
needles or teeth
broken pipes
backhoes
inside the ceiling
where trance-phenomena
grow wax-like
left to their

elected habitual condition
always at odds
yet for the agent intellect
free and objective
why spend money on it—
old ones open mouths
young ones gather there
resentments begin to show
inside
unknown opuscula
as shot hits car
her knee gets torn up
a little
in a pale place
by an iron bridge
and a white church
and a left turn lane
adjusted to compensate
for the unusual perspective
applied or inherent
adjusted for the slope of the hill
wooded hill to low stream
high boots
kingfisher
omniform forms
indelible syllables
strung through
the plenum's
glow

draw hither
ionosphere
extend forearm
mark formulation
I was that I
that was yesterday
these are minute features
that characterize me
while I bend back
your finger
in perfect awareness
of the mystical winds
called flesh

AN ANALYSIS

The property of each occupies its own house. Salt clings to the fruit on their tables. It was none other than the sun itself came roaring down at this time. Slanting toward the west its influence dried up the benign moisture conferred by the east. All three went walking before supper and there was in consequence devised an orderly allocation of graves; they were to be placed side by side where daylight dims and trees lean low against hearts of stone. Later their postprandial conference gave rise to conflict. Would those dispositions become timely? Throughout the night the hesitant one assessed the evidence; the others stared at the trombones. We know what becomes active when we sleep—yet that was missing. At last the dewless dawn signaled a first attainment, when their molecules spontaneously unwove: for the state they sought could never have succumbed to them so long as they had clung to material mediation. Now the morning air shot through the framework events contrived and they were no longer bound by the concepts that bore them. They could stretch and swarm into all physical dimensions or pour themselves into every object of thought. Shining out of the stillness where they once had lurked, the sun became the organ of their efficacy.

POIMANDRES

clear away a space for *fresh water*
jumping from the sky
we who nothing can
distinguish from no one
be near or be
near us now be recognizable
who foreknew this rain
so refined—
nightly inundation
in adobo
impalpable
had you been present
some mortal's share
would have turned away
from the greased footpath
arms folded
unentered into this state
to stare
with a sleepwalker's
ochre eye
through the sodden heat
behind the wall where
nothing originates
nothing terminates
the wall is a vegetable
wailing on high

blue and immobile
a kind of breakfast
in its mouth
so luminous
the discharge
go
    wipe the blood off
I notice your skin vanishes
while my lamp burns all night long
what is the indispensable condition
linking these two—
some fibrous base
that chokes the spine
or great disheveled dome lit up
by Artifice
the nerveless old snake
whack it
thou
empty sign

There is a case to be made for listing things about which we do not care. A point of confusion arises regarding order, where order is nothing save a faint posthumous beat signifying—*what* today? Signifying both. Both an intensity armed against slackness, and a stylish meandering near boundaries. Not like this. Stages of avowal are managed consecutively, if state law allows. Many older organisms tend to be self-governing, and no amount of reflection can unscrew the basic template for their embittered sentience. Which brings us to hatred, its causes and how to remove them. Predisposed to calm, we turn imprudently toward resentment, anger, and indifference. Or toward those who think in such terms. I can't address them here and now as I might wish, nor can I say I would do so if I were actually able to—not out of hesitation or weakness, but because I'm looking for a vale to wander in, a vale of views enjoyed as much for their beauty and sweep, as for their way of adapting themselves to states we can inhabit simply by bending our knees. And once having found it, I won't return. There the morning skies glow, clothes fit well, statutes cooperate. The river distributes itself without reference to those who walk beside it, and the debris it carries is pledged.

FOR THE LAWFUL HEIRS

the people in question
dig quietly
with festal fork
and feather
a pause
means nothing
perhaps privilege
working its way back
to shore
the case of driftwood
truly stated
or peculations of
appellants
at 9 a.m.
silver car
moon-shaped
entrance marked
customer
coots
dive
kinglets
flicker

TOWER ROAD

Matter is a fog one looks through toward pale headlights, while the pavement reveals certain weaknesses to be resolved by wishing, regretting, or despairing. Ignorance and doubt maintain matter's interest in us, over fresh surfaces winding east, through rocks and plastic cups, to the incandescent threshold—where all is puréed into a single featureless face the moment life concludes. A clean car delivers our nutriment, the cloud jewel, the ice jewel. Those who make little noise or whose abode is immeasurably distant are presumed to have escaped the prison of earth, impasturing the sky. They whitewash the white rooms. Footprints slide from their feet. Sometimes they drink juice from trees.

MORNING SUTTA

flying limpid
bramble drop

verdant nebbe
of two *tartari*

startled bright
concrete stair

2

BIG SHIP

whoever comes tonight
must express what happens
when a substance is endowed
with speeds approaching the end state
of what thought aspires to—
our technicians can read oatmeal
and parse illustrative examples
into huge asphalt snakes
intertwining among minds
partially corrected for
vindictive indicators
hence no reaction can
express one thing above
all others—is that spider
a threat to your perfection
its being rightly strives
to pluck this window
in gray light the blue form
is lowered into its infinite
self-sufficiency
suppose then we are
at rest centered in the thing's
brain perfectly happy there
or else suspended in the brain
of a distant object
it clearly follows that

whatever we conclude has
spent month after month
inside a simpleton
Lord I hear that that
which happens to us
outside the usual course
thinks we can change
let us pay homage to what
is not really a statement
proof appended here
which has tried to connect
motley to colorless when
you spread your whistle against
this enormous space place
your finger in the clouds
and drink in the tincture
of a clear and effective exhalation
respecting the dead who sailed
on a big ship five centuries
ago last night when questions arose
such as why enveilings or lustrate
subsumptions should follow
immediately flip feigning
to seduce some other verb
that doesn't break down
from non-perception—say
upstanding oracles of what
splendor must this be
this legitimate get up

uptake shatter erected
to oneself this stinging
mirabile with adjustments
enough to quiet them
in a crazy burst of sun
the mole will penetrate
to what is ominously
washed by a stream

I saw my self the other night, loosely framed, having given up, having discarded, having been freed from, my own multiplicity. And I saw the luminous whiteness of the sky contained in my own hands, and fell asleep in this formless place and could not be evicted.

FOR DALLY KIMOKO

Who forgets to perfect enjoyment flakes apart from the force of a will to fail. After which, claims encumber thought. They cause the phone to be handed to her, into which she speaks, then hands it to me, and I speak, then a voice speaks, then several voices speak, and a shadow breaks apart. To be valid, this episode must be imputed to those who are absent. Then all prior states must vanish before the next phase can begin. But why be anxious? Why care about what else could be possible when the true goal involves having all our senses register every aspect of physical existence constantly and unremittingly? Such an attainment would fill up our hearts without resorting to paradox. Any estimated shortfall would still leave adequate amounts set aside to satisfy our need not to fluctuate. Even a dog knows this. A happy, inquisitive, spontaneous dog, *eating hungrily*. When in the future a kind of perpetual hum is heard, which grows louder as temperatures rise, strong hands will take command and clear light will darken us. At night a heavy body will be thrown against the floor and a tambourine will vibrate.

AGRICULTURAL BAROMETER

like mercury rising in a stick
of
full body armor
roar in my face little airless sound

THE WILL

It dreamt that it spoke as it dreamt and wrote down what it spoke in echoes of situations dreamt about which its mind wondered at. There's a quality about it however that did not involve any dreaming (as far as could be determined, no one being in a position to grasp either the nature of this quality or the experience whereby its existence was inferred). Those echoes it knew were clean. Then swooping-in thought incapable of economy began to vary over time. Which might also be said of silence were it not the right affect babe—for if mind were not itself object and were not freely described as all things and all things differently seen or felt, noting in particular a bed of stones overlaid by straight lines babe, then this would not appear as manipulation or surveillance but a clear fountain of flowing tongues—not memory of non-existence but an orderly disposition of meanings and events. While still functioning let us all be ambient zero in what We Heap. Our acts are ignorant of their purposes. With closed eyes, we watch the waters overrun the fields. Would it have been wrong to have given access to an unauthorized discussion—or what passed for a discussion, sixteen present four voices heard and an undetermined number listening —just when incentives should have been sought to ignore it? Or lug it around like a dirty price. Who advises the teeth, the hair, and the gums? Who ascribes to the abyss humility? Appetite is resigned to wait it out. Mind is tautological. But dreams sputter all night long. Nothing can be moderated by will, only by circumstance, in which the will is one element.

TREASURE HIDDEN SINCE

the state would
gather up
soft tissue
like wildflowers
at the plow
meditating
bell-like
they flew

the leaf
the flake
the filament

TRUST IS THE NAME

OF THE FATHER

I found myself informing the court that *these* particular shoes were actually alive. That night voices puckered the wall. I reached inside my throat and felt for scars.

HALLUCINATION BLUES

Great floods ring the bell singing *thy time is come* to be unbound
while inside the bell a fight ensues and a mixed attitude
leans back into abating showers. The head lacks a face.
The skin replaces itself without changing its nature.

Tranquility withdraws, to be reached by a bridge
that vanishes each day as the sun comes up
and investors make fists out of forfeits
no one avows, deriving them

from a deep gorge of purified conceptions.

Meanwhile, spirits are forbidden to move
absent payment of percentage rent
that would have been due
had they stayed put and clung to their anxiety

stretching across the water like a train.

HALLUCINATION

This (historical) object has decided to exist obliquely and by virtue of its existence to become correlated with the approaches taken to it by diverse groups of object-beholders—constituents—who appear motivated in their actions by a hunger for possession, or by the opposite impulse to escape from themselves into what they see. Dredging up strange but deeply felt emotions, they apply them directly to the screen—which is gray and framed by burnt plastic. One pushes it aside like a shadow. Austere but fragrant (redolent) the object branches down stairways, through hallways, out doorways, along streets and rivers until, carried away by birds, it is allocated over numberless empty landscapes. Out of its dispersion new objects are confected, to be placed side by side, on a mountain meadow, while a backward-looking daylight wanes, and the hand recedes that grasps the string stretching away to the great dead images of the past. I reach toward them from the present. How is it thinking of them, transparent or ashen, implausible then and now, arranged in the casual order of assumed routines, unconsciously shuffling through the days that bore them and that they came to represent as signs conceived to recoup an intensity and splendor that defined some prior synthesis—how is it by occult operation ordinary things occur? Whose present with its 'here' is here? Who drinks nectar through a nail?

THE ELIXIR

Pull this rope to relieve symptoms
from harsh to mellow the
growth scare all been dreading
and swaps themselves tutelary
update deficiency tabs
        and
        I'll be sure to
    prune my eyelids

from within polymorphous shadows
steel stairs lead up an embankment
and my thought is to climb them
accompanied by Prester John
our voices fall
like pallets from a truck
two pigeons
pivot in an invisible maze

then one day I got a call

wandering barefoot

into crosshairs

followed by
a trickle

seen from above
unkempt phyla

in deciduous
enclosures

lift bar and pull
he said

send forth froth
or tint to glimmer

through fleshy
smoke drifting

halfway down
the classic age

of limestone
whose swollen magi

traverse your sheath
finding an inmost

sore point
by derivative force

springs upward
notwithstanding

the lightning chain
bound him

precariously
to *spiritum arcanum*

sprouting inside
our caravan

fallen again
to its daily limit

the rug masters
tied up

with nylon strings
winding down

the mountain
like trained

animals
their dark

square feet
amending the path

while he
rides on

fingers
crystallized

the red wagon
goes boom

such fatal
consciousness

our specialty
said the duck

slung over
his back

behold
seven signs

for seven
planets

floating like
incrustations

of tongue-
ready gold

or telltale
iridium

then impulse
is ushered in

and walls
cut open

to admit
pure figure

stretched out
on a scintillant

shadow
undimmed

undefined
strumming away

in what form
the otiose hedge it

below each
day's excess

an impredicable
blank

lying awake
in fidelity

to a distant
site beside

a small pond
a flock

whips left
leafless tree

not anticipating
a drop

reverses it in
faint light

tremulous
straddles—

truth was
he'd been

stricken
blood sport

for lease
ground-rent

owed by consociation
of idiosyncrasies

sated with tamarind
soup or lack

of institutional
fortitude

after one week
ghosts ribbon

through
the torpor

upsprung
southbound

cyclones
indifferent

which items
to devastate

when sun
bleeds

air falls
below earth

solemn companions
otherwise

estranged their
temperaments fuse

in one ecstatic
movement

we put on
our yellow vests

and wade out
into the heat

of an intense
transfiguration

glancing back
without remembering

EL POETA

The latter possesses only transitory instincts, parts of which are snapped off to form stars. *Anabaptist*. To the east the lake floats above the grass. *Acervation*. Below the surface, the present me is preserved forever, while the former me is cut off. *Ya-ho-bo*. Dipping my hand in, I watch the cold fluid shrink my fingers, which represent five lines composed with first stress off, second stress on, and .03 percent overlap.

Complete silence, then its opposite—for the moment, Teacher says, they are one, like a trumpet.

3

REMEMBERING WHAT

I (SHOULD) KNOW

For the period of thirty lunar days after the receipt of appropriate notice [undefined], the parties [not specified] shall attempt in good faith to resolve whatever dispute has (evidently) arisen by employing the *advanced measurement approach*, which computes a given event's penumbra as it tumbles into the lap of someone who studies it. In theory, we do this once a year, when the window cracks open to let in frost, or the broad floating disk hides in summer grass, or the whitewashed darkness drifts by. Reject the astringent, my advice to you, lay out the clothes you will need for the next round, gross up the flow of bodies moving both directions, then subtract the interdicted ones. Arbitration would be an alternative were it not chained to *arbitrary*, which sits beside it on the swings near the cliff. Exactly what is the 'tone' provided for contractually? How does its transfer take place in absence of a transferor? Should we attribute an outbreak of modifications and amendments to figures we can't see, even though tastes in figures have changed, and now the most striking thing about them, to us, is the prominence of their teeth? Why can't my right hand block out the sun? In the stillness of possibility is *nothing* described?

53

HOPE FOR HAPPINESS

The diffused responsibility of the approval process means it is more than likely that you will make an uninformed choice. Reviewing accounts is work—generally tedious work—and if you are not familiar with it, difficult work, thankless work, lingering and vexatious work, aggravating, terrible. So you are tempted to rely on others, even on those who have mastered information they can use against you, or who try to fix in you the uncomfortable feeling that your own thoughts are ashamed of you—or who can demonstrate that a premonition of your death has accrued inside statements like 'I think I'm right.' You who cannot bear to see a fly killed, whose *ingenuity, openness, and plain expression* make you a joy to your heirs, who reap their hopes from your testament, devising hay for a chest, pumpkin seeds for eyes, and clouds for cleft lids—you descend to a floor fabricated from things that have burst. Because it makes no sense to proceed, you remain still, only turning your head toward the east then to the west then back again. In either direction the objects seen—buildings, streetlights, windows, cars—fall away at a constant rate of speed, which seems to increase slightly the instant you shift your eyes. Someone crosses the floor in front of you. There's a rhythm and buoyancy in this passage, as though obliviousness has become insight. On the street stick figures trudge through the snow, and pause under laden awnings. You struggle to exclude the entire scene from your existence, or else to suspend its vesting indefinitely. But the power of alienation soaks you in flames.

HYPOTHECARY TRANSACTION

There is something conceptually primitive about the problems bequeathed to us. Those problems admit of a twofold division: the rational and the intuitive. Either or both will be swallowed up in the state of *nothing whatever* if we are lucky enough to reach it. To demonstrate this we run the engine backwards: a rooster and three hens are standing on the tracks—watch as they pass into a wholly indefinite state. Inside the shed the air trembles and repents, so you conclude that an entire human being is smaller than a snail. As the door shuts, reason reasons its form and those of its collateral components peeling. Nothing will not *not* happen because of this: it is simply an exercise in internal refinement or an adjustment to basis. What then really occurred ten years ago? Were they negligent or devious? Do the same facts imply both? To answer this we roll the engine forward without starting it. The words "attain" and "dwell" are then read through the wheels as they pass over them so that "at" and "we" intimate the lost cave of intuition far inside the brain. *We* are now *at* the place we share with it and it with us. But redemption is not consented to. Mistakes continue to spill over the land as an affront to pure thought. Adventurers reorganize in ever-growing numbers. We wait uneasily as they come to us. End of poem.

BLOOD RED ROSES

Reason spots the resemblance between emptiness and the progressive rendering of an aura. For several years now I have considered words and phrases in isolation, but have fallen short in being able to construe what they mean. While I judge this failure a failure of skill, whatever the character of that skill, or who should be its possessor, I move along to the next zone, lured by chimes. Behind me, the eye and the ear form themselves into a matrix out of which time exhibits specific modes. There are six modes in all. Three are illimitable. One is formless. Start with that. In the pleasant light of glossy skin I view everything in hindsight. The mystery that brings me to this moment cultivates a feeling of persistence that stretches out for examination before it flutters away. Things that no longer exist labor to find the place where words turn into thoughts and thoughts turn into people. Instinct counsels against talking to them. Their faces and bodies are changing in ways I can't follow. When I'm gone they're still here, but they're different, more aggressive, more acquisitive, impatiently acquiescent in third-party efforts to fund them. Inside daylight a false daylight waits, and they are drawn to it. They have no power to retain their own structure, and have been advised that this is the case. They eat burnt flies' wings and bed down on diatoms. Overlooking their lunar otherness, I catch glimpses of sandy shapes, walking or crawling. Beyond them, whalefish blow, and I see a cold gem ripening.

FLAMING

More numbness from less pain, I heard the preacher say. When does apprehension become extinction? Of what omitted act is it the fruit? We walked steadily toward the bright red buildings, as winds cut through the easement and the guard station caught fire. Awake now, we began to conform our limbs to an independence that had always eluded us, hidden away by the back door—this we hoped to maintain, striking a pure path through the floating blossoms. That we sank almost at once was not a surprise, oppressed as we were by thick roots. Over time we lost the taste of disappointment, or ceased to be immobilized by it. The trees spread out and their vast branches calmed us. We shut our eyes and imagined all possible future states, including those accelerated by commutation, those unwound by substitution, compared their anticipated effects, judged how they might differ according to the scrutiny they drew. From a common starting point, we followed the most absurd strands wherever they led, on flights of extreme complexity, or down long descents to a weariness we embraced as a bulwark against further motion. [*For the record, doubt was introduced at this point.*]

SECRECY OFFICER

When pressure is applied to agents, servants, entities, or subsidiary entities by means of demands, reckonings, bonds, or inducements, the resulting frisson is barely contained. Thus the term 'release.' The need to price these alternatives offsets the dilation of simple desire. Can one even breathe without escaping this hive? Stillness and remoteness are worth sustaining, until they cloy. Change in the usual sense is obliterated: once synonymous with time, today it signifies parallel auxiliary states untenably elided by squinting. When nothingness is acquired, failure to meet contractual terms is assured. Transferring this exposure to a poppet brings relief, but hinders care. Down in the ghostly streets fog moistens every footprint. Where the lake had been there now stands an obelisk. The pavement begins to sway, giving a greenish tint to nearby objects, which turn silver as they recede—for as the swaying intensifies everything grows more and more distant, and one's own vantage point slowly but perceptibly deteriorates, until it slumps into the earth. 'Shadows catch an alien motion,' writes the secrecy officer on the lost page in front of him.

MIWA-SAN

The game is played in the black snow amid pieces of street-corner garbage.[1] In steep morning shadows, human and non-human forms place themselves in various positions according to an intricate, almost incomprehensible pattern derived from the day's paper—few realize the pattern can be readily grasped by closing one's left eye, and lifting one's right eye toward the sun. No strategy *per se* is necessary although participants may prohibit by general announcement certain pre-designated actions if they so choose. By this means they can anticipate and defend against strategies devised by others, should anyone feel the need either to devise or defend (almost no one ever does). Each participant must demonstrate a minimum level of skill, and is liable for any loss resulting from hesitancy in applying that skill. As the game begins, preliminary data circulate along the wet pavement, over curbs, between cars, under tires, down drains. Occasionally data warp from the force of the participants' speech, or from the intense charges emitted by the participants' stares. Painstakingly acquired mastery converts these data into great storehouses from which key details are chosen for constructing vignettes, following the process described in the Participant's Guide. Every storehouse occupies a contrary position relative to every other storehouse, with the ultimate effect being that all the vignettes cancel one another out. Despite this,

1. Unwritten rules can be found close by; while they are strictly applied, they nonetheless allow for sudden variations, deviations, discrepancies, adjustments, extenuations. After years of careful observing, participants are able to internalize them.

they exert in the aggregate a strange, unfocused power, enabling participants to forge second-order, derivative vignettes. These in turn disclose puzzling vistas in which each detail has been replaced by a new, apparently unrelated one; a torn shoelace, for example, substitutes for a rolled up copy of this week's *Barron's*. Thus every creative act is an involuntary delegation, consistent with the goal of the game. Miwa-san describes this goal as securing 'the realistically appraised prospect of increased returns from any given activity.' Returns therefore are not paramount, only the 'realistic' appraisal of their potential. But if no one keeps score, there is always the risk of having your head split open from improper technique.

ZOMBIELAND

in return for which
it was misread as 'love *of* nothing'—typical of the submerged will
to carve everything away until a manikin is revealed or a wire-
frame figure offering itself to whatever acts or constructions are
held necessary to carry us on to the next junction, or back to the
switchyard, where similar items appear, each with small decisive
differences that tend to reverberate below sea level, and eventually
locate themselves between the concepts of anxiety and unpre-
dictability. While there is a formal choice to be made, at this point
the sounds of the absent children's voices, and the rain coming
down, provoke an adjournment. The institution waits for us out
front; but we leave through the back, skirting the frog pond. In
view of our finite commitment to total confinement we become
watchful, marking how the rain rides the blossoms into the grass
under which old years sleep. But these thoughts are interrupted by
a large sibyl carrying a blank sheet of paper. The paper is held up
high and both sides shown, then laid flat on the conference room
table. 'The raindrops on the window resemble deceased insects,'
someone notes, and this observation is categorized under *licen-
tiousness* in the left-hand column, which seems to have drawn itself
when no one was looking. Another blank sheet is produced, this
one an inverted copy of the first—we wait to see if writing will ap-
pear. To distract us, the sibyl turns her face to the wall and begins
to sob. The manikin rolls forward to reprimand or console her, we
can't tell which because a fog has intervened, briefly restricting our
access to our own senses. Then sixteen pairs of eyes peer in at the

doorway, tied to the mast of an implacable urge for absolute accuracy of apprehension, evidenced by their simultaneous blinking. The second sheet has meanwhile become a great delirious tome. From a distance it looks like a code of some kind or a set of statutes, complete with multiple numbered sections, subsections, and subsubsections, appended to a vast preamble which purports to define each term used therein. The preamble is approximately three times the length of what it precedes and things are growing inside. Suddenly a shrill cry calls us back to the scene of our previous adjournment, which exploded during our absence. The walls now have strips of carpet tacked on to them, and stunned people are walking up and down. They peel off in groups of two and reach for their phones. As the air floods with blank sheets, insects come back to life for their final ascent. Lovelorn in the shade, the sibyl dreams of her inorganic twin sister, postponing the inevitable entrance of *one word* that flashes on and off like a beacon. Above the great meadow sheer contraries change places without end. Pulling back or pulling away cannot be an option, not because it would be hard to admit failure, or to confess our inability to finish the job, whatever the job finally turns out to be, but because it never occurs to anyone. And this will always be the case. The present and future are in complementary position, shining nowhere but in the dark, so to speak, while fears muster inside the sentences sent to calm them.

HIGH STILLNESS

for Jeremy

abandoned sugar plague
was the size of a spoon
lighted inside from without
all components blended

with a lovely intimate
becoming harder to see
or loose pile of stones
each addressed distinctly

along the pilgrimage
to indemnification
eels dressed in white
stokers heaters pumps

ridiculous borrowed beams
dumped over our clothes
we were face to face
I stood there freezing

hoists chutes ducts doors
everyone fears a word
there is no equity
once the wall turns blue

generally subliminal oppression
fails to produce benefit
as the soul dies
all merge together

carpets screens awnings
all that magnificence
here skips whither
nothing else is

but vivid flesh
to attorn bodies
intending to be born
by termination

we bequeath to you
brute aperitif
lunatic air vents
depletion recapture

and sheaves of waves
shall be raised up
whole slices of them
simmer in the sky

glad plight can ye
allocate roughly
what no one lisps
to be distributed

incrementally
which this supplements
extra-contractually
if suspected to exist

I remember
the trees the hill
the rain
the weeds the stones

the great dogmatic
inhibitory functions
where they met
north of zero

peacefully appending
serrated distaff
to anonymous
spasm

an unfelt blow
a crust
or scurf
or filament

an exalted act
in reference to
a spent
standard

the imposition
of a sluice
or opalescent
zigzag

through headstones
repelling
daylight
in whose name

splendid automata
are hanged
Walter Map
extracted them

eating milkweed
on dry toast
flecked
with poppies

PSYCHOLOGICAL ETHICS

Recently we have been collecting all kinds of concepts and boiling them down to one or two. Our old approach was to try to quantify uncertainties, which led to our eventual recognition that quantifying uncertainties only increased our perplexity. Today we undertake no operation other than simple elimination, setting aside time-honored rules of thumb. The specimen concepts, meanwhile, build up a makeshift picture whose outlines are to be studied when neglect of them becomes physically painful. We match up these outlines with what can be supported by a process consisting of, say, eighteen identifiable steps, each documented by its own small drawing of a table and a chair. Over time our sensations learn how to mimic sensations; we begin to focus on instants of pure movement to the exclusion of all else—for example when the pumice shoots past us out the door. Returning to our tasks, we now engage in open colloquies where statements are not dismissed out of hand, but are taken at due weight for their transformative properties—properties relished for the leverage they apply to ordinary actors and events, so that one basic phrase can be spread over the entire plane of representation. *The problem with all this is not that it's too abstract, but that it's not abstract enough.* We have no issue with the desire to remove impediments; we share that as a goal in fact. Our concern revolves around the idea that impediments force themselves on us because we have lost our sense of their purpose, which was always related to their remaining undetected through an entire cycle. But somewhere inside a truth grates. We can affirm whatever we like about any given state of affairs. We can claim that we are who we are and we act as we act because the system is stable, although subject to shocks. In so doing, we confess that what we describe is no longer linked to what we observe. Does each of us (therefore) remain a different thing, or is each of us many things with the will to be one thing—and is that one the whole of what it is, or isn't?

THE BLACK MAZE

money draws money
appalled by dust
more of that excess
nudges me aside

after death
a lazy tune
the sandy surface
looks edible

drift with me
easy at first
then abundant
perspiration

when spouts jam
which philosopher
matters most
are angels pitiful

the peeling paint
and atrocious necessity
do you think
of starlight

abrogating
a dead lease
pirata
swimming

stray pencil marks
are not present
in these paintings
of trees

apricot skin
of our quite
invisible
flower

and why does
my head
fish up
loose strata

a time to be
liquid
seasoned
slow

or
melting
rock-bound
comprehension

or the sway
of seedfield
sunlight
bathes

somehow
had foretold
ulterior
symmetry

the undescried
irritation
weakens me
how to explain

am I
or of this
a strangeness
the appointed time

cloven echo
clearly states
though dimmer
care for this

its picture
shows us
on foot
sad to arrive

bone-white
series three
psyche
lines the shore

the brick steps
are leaving
Côte d'Ivoire
by parabola

or perhaps
per stirpes
the aliment
clutched

slantwise
breaded
with snow
Selah

bronze needles
sighing
like feathers
in trees

bless his
winged heart
he is a
sea captain

icicles form
on dead tissue's
thousandfold
fringes

to rejoice
means
no revulsion
is felt

galvanic
subsidy
conveys
no relief

no reason
to buy
from thieves
self-enlightened

she ran back
to the car
rain held off
she was reborn

but exposure
persists
revered
and crystalline

THE CIRCUIT

Several times a day someone passes by the door holding a report. It appears to be the same person moving in the same direction each time, so I infer that there may be a circuit involved. Over the course of the day, each time the person passes, I notice the report has grown in size from the last time. I also notice the person's walking speed appears to have slowed. Because I'm never actually watching when this happens—but only catching brief glimpses almost after the fact—I am unable to surmise much about these circuits except the slowing of speed and lengthening of report. This activity persists well beyond the length of a normal day, for the window has darkened and brightened several times—actually more than several—as the person continues to slow, and the report continues to grow. What strikes me as particularly frustrating is that no matter how slowly the person moves, and no matter how unwieldy the report has become, I am never alert enough to manage more than a hasty, belated glance toward the door. So for example, whether the person is a man or woman, or even a person at all, I can't tell. Likewise I don't know whether the report represents words or numbers, or some combination of them; or if words, in what language. Or perhaps the report manifests some other category of inscription beyond words or numbers, if indeed the marks on the report are meant to be intelligible? These problems only increase with the extreme slowness that now characterizes each traverse. The slower the progress, the more difficult it is to grasp it clearly. I can't imagine how someone moving so slowly can so successfully evade my apprehension unless there is in reserve an incredible speed to be applied the instant my sensing is sensed. Eventually I turn away from the documents in front of me, and focus only on the act of observing. I wait and wait: for at the last circuit, the window had darkened and brightened countless times at the very moment of passage—the imperceptible soul had appeared to be absolutely still, and the report had grown to the size of a planet.

WILLIAM FULLER

was raised in Barrington, Illinois, and studied
literature at Lawrence University and the
University of Virginia. His most recent books
of poetry include *Sadly* (2003) and *Watchword*
(2006). He is chief fiduciary officer of the
Northern Trust Company in Chicago.